CONTENTS

FOREWORD

My journey into the Catholic Church was progressing smoothly. One by one, I found answers to my Protestant objections to Catholicism. I came to believe in the Eucharist, the Papacy, Apostolic Succession, and Scripture's teaching that both faith and works are needed for salvation. The key to my conversion was to stop trusting whatever Protestant authors and preachers said about Catholicism and start reading what the Catholic Church said about herself. I scoured the Church Fathers and discovered that the early Christian Church was undeniably *Catholic*. Uncovering one doctrinal jewel after another, I was well on my way to becoming a Catholic. Then, I encountered Mary and came to a screeching halt.

Mary was the hardest of all Catholic doctrines for me to accept. Many things about Mary didn't make sense to my Protestant way of thinking. I called my seminary friend, Scott Hahn, who had recently become a Catholic. I agonized to Scott, "Mary is *really* hard to understand." Scott encouraged me, "Yes, but the hardest is the best." So I persevered until I finally grasped the central truths about Mary.

Mary is one of the most precious treasures within Catholicism. Discovering the truths about Mary requires perseverance, but accepting her will change your life forever. She will enrich your relationship with Christ in unimaginable ways. One of my greatest privileges as a Catholic has been to publicly honor Jesus' mother. I am astounded at the abundant blessings Jesus bestows upon those who do so.

Reading, studying, and digesting the contents of this gem-packed booklet, *Beginning Apologetics 6: How to Explain and Defend Mary*, will equip you to bring honor to Mary. Nearly all of us have friends and family members who have questions about Mary that this booklet can help answer. Many prospective converts to Catholicism are just waiting for someone to explain Mary to them in a clear and simple way. That someone can be you. You don't need to be an expert to help them; you just need to master the facts in this practical handbook.

I highly recommend the entire *Beginning Apologetics* series, but I especially like this booklet. *Beginning Apologetic 6* is a useful, understandable, and extremely valuable tool that will enable you to become a blessing to those searching for the fullness of the Faith.

—STEVE WOOD

Former Presbyterian minister
Founder of Family Life Center, International

INTRODUCTION TO MARY

We Catholics cherish our Marian beliefs. We recognize that the privileges God gave the Blessed Virgin Mary are gifts for the whole human race. We believe our Marian doctrines are based solidly on public revelation. We also see our many beautiful Marian devotions as a practical way of living out what Sacred Scripture and Sacred Tradition teach about our Blessed Mother.

However, for many non-Catholics Mary is a huge stumbling block. They think Catholics "make too much of Mary," that we give her too much attention, taking away from the honor we owe to Christ. As one anti-Catholic writer put it: "This most blessed of women, the mother of Jesus, is thus made His chief rival and competitor for the loyalty and devotion of the human heart."[1]

As evangelists, it's our job to show non-Catholics that Mary and Jesus are not in competition, but are members of the same team. We must share the obvious truth that Mary is the first and best Christian who only leads us closer to her Son, Jesus. We must assure them that Mary's privileges come exclusively from God and reflect His love and mercy. Finally, we must invite them to discover how Mary's role in salvation is taught from Genesis to Revelation and she is, by God's design, the spiritual mother of all Christians.

We have designed this handbook to:

(1) Show the solid biblical basis for Catholic Marian beliefs.
(2) Explain and defend the four defined Marian doctrines.
(3) Answer the common objections Catholics receive about Mary.

We hope this booklet will help Catholics and non-Catholics appreciate Mary's tremendous role in salvation history and to embrace her as Jesus intended: as their spiritual mother.

---

[1] Lorraine Boettner, *Roman Catholicism* (Phillipsburg, NJ: Presbyterian and Reformed Publishing, 1962), 146.

MARY AND SACRED SCRIPTURE

TYPOLOGY

The Old Testament (OT) prepared the way for the New Testament (NT). Persons and events in the OT prefigured, foreshadowed, anticipated, and symbolized persons and events in the NT. According to an ancient Christian saying: "the New Testament lies hidden in the Old and the Old Testament is unveiled in the New" (*Catechism of the Catholic Church* [hereafter *CCC*], 129).

The OT persons and events are called "types" of the NT persons and events they prefigure. A type is a prophetic foreshadowing of its NT counterpart.

> **To fully understand the Old Testament we must read it in terms of types.**

The *CCC* has a brief but excellent section on OT types in numbers 128–130.

To fully understand the OT we must read it in terms of types. Typology shows many NT doctrines, including Mary's privileges, clearly revealed in the OT. Once a non-Catholic understands the meaning and importance of OT types, he will discover that *all* Catholic beliefs about Mary are found in the Bible.

The NT *requires* that we read the OT in a typological sense.[2] Consider:

(1) In Matthew 12:40, Jesus teaches that Jonah's three days in the belly of the great fish foreshadowed Jesus' three days in the tomb.

(2) In John 3:14, Jesus says that the bronze serpent of Numbers 21:9 symbolized His crucifixion.

(3) In 1 Peter 3:19–21, St. Peter points out that the flood in the time of Noah prefigured Christian baptism.

(4) In 1 Corinthians 10:4, St. Paul calls the rock that followed the Israelites in the desert "Christ." Notice he does not say the rock was *like* Christ; St. Paul says the rock *was* Christ. He uses this language to stress that the relationship between a type and its NT fulfillment is more than a similarity.

(5) In Romans 5:14, St. Paul specifically calls Adam a type of Christ.

These examples show how the NT teaches that in the OT persons and events, we are to see doctrines that are made more explicit in the gospel. Thus, to be faithful to the NT, we should seek to appreciate the rich typology found in the OT.

There are three major OT types of Mary: Eve, the Ark of the Covenant, and the Queen Mother. These three types of Mary support all our Marian beliefs.

---

2 Obviously, we must first read the Bible in a literal sense. All the other senses of Scripture—typological, moral, and analogical—are based upon the literal. See *CCC*, 115–118.

MARY AS THE SECOND EVE

As they studied the Bible, the early Church Fathers made rich use of typology. Romans 5:14 teaches that Adam was a type of Christ. The Fathers realized other individuals involved in the Fall had NT counterparts. The devil, a fallen angel, brought words of death to Eve; the angel Gabriel brought words of life to Mary. Eve, our mother in the flesh, disobeyed God and cooperated greatly in Adam's sin, which caused the fall of the human race. Mary obeyed God and contributed greatly to Christ's redemptive mission. She was his mother and perfect disciple.

"The knot of Eve's disobedience was loosed by the obedience of Mary."
—St. Irenaeus

The Fathers made the obvious connection: as Christ is the new Adam (1 Corinthians 15:45), Mary is the new Eve. After Adam and Eve had sinned, Genesis 3:15 prophesies a woman and her son who will be at total enmity with the serpent (Satan) and his descendents:

> "I will put enmity between you and the woman, and between your offspring and hers; He will strike at your head, while you strike at his heel" (*New American Bible*).

The woman's son will crush the serpent's head. Since the man who crushes the serpent's head is obviously Jesus, the woman must be Mary.

Thus, Genesis 3:15–17 describes two teams: the fall team—Adam and Eve, and the redemption team—Jesus and Mary, the new Adam and new Eve. The earliest Church Fathers, such as St. Justin and St. Irenaeus,[3] were quick to realize this. Although the human race fell through Adam, Eve's role was crucial. Jesus redeemed the human race, but Mary's role was likewise crucial. As we will see in the following section, Sacred Scripture continually shows *Jesus and Mary together* in the pivotal events of our salvation.

Jesus and Mary Together *Crush Satan's head.*

A quick overview of the Bible confirms that Jesus and Mary *together* will crush Satan's head. Notice how the OT describes women (types of Mary) who crush Israel's enemies (types of Satan). In Judges 4:17–22, Jael drives a tent peg through the skull of the Canaanite general, Sisera. Judges 5:24 celebrates her: "*Most blessed of women be Jael.*"

---

[3] "Just as [Eve] … having become disobedient, was made the cause of death for herself and for the whole human race; so also Mary, … being obedient, was made the cause of salvation for herself and the whole human race. … Thus, the knot of Eve's disobedience was loosed by the obedience of Mary. What the virgin Eve had bound in unbelief, the virgin Mary loosed through faith." (St. Irenaeus, *Against Heresies*, 3,22,4; Jurgens, Volume 1, #224.)

"[Jesus] became Man by the virgin so that the course which was taken by disobedience in the beginning through the agency of the serpent, might be also the very course by which it would be put down. For Eve, a virgin and undefiled, conceived the word of the serpent, and bore disobedience and death. But the virgin Mary received faith and joy when the angel Gabriel announced to her the glad tidings…. And she replied: 'Be it done unto me according to thy word.'" (St. Justin Martyr, *Dialogue with Trypho the Jew*, 100; Jurgens, Volume 1, #141.)

Judges 9:50–55 describes a woman who drops a millstone on the head of tyrannical King Abimelech, fracturing his skull. Judith delivers the Jewish people from the Assyrian army by beheading its commander-in-chief, Holofernes, with his own sword as he slept (Judith 12–13). Judith's heroism is celebrated with the words:

> "*you are blessed* by the Most High God *above all women on earth*; and blessed be the Lord God … who has guided you to strike the *head* of the leader of our enemies" (Judith 13:18).

The praises of Jael and Judith both anticipate Elizabeth's praise of Mary in Luke 1:42, "*Blessed are you among women.*" Notice that Elizabeth connects Mary with Jesus by immediately adding, "and blessed is the fruit of your womb!"

Righteous men also crushed heads in the OT. David (a type of Jesus, who is the son of David) defeated the Philistine champion Goliath and chopped off his head with the giant's own sword (1 Samuel 17:41–58). In the OT, types of both Mary and Jesus (the woman and her seed) are shown crushing types of Satan.

Jesus definitively crushed Satan's head on Calvary.[4] Significantly, all four evangelists record that Calvary means "skull-place." Satan intended to strike Jesus a lethal blow on the cross, but it proved to be a minor wound ("you strike at his heel"). Satan suffered the mortal wound ("he will strike at your head") as Jesus destroyed the power of sin and death.

Who was at Christ's side on Calvary? Mary. What does Jesus call her? "*Woman.*" Mary is the New Eve. She is the "woman" of Genesis 3:15, the "woman" of John 2 whose intercession at Cana launched Christ's public ministry, the "woman" of John 19 at the foot of the cross, and the "woman" of Revelation 12 who, with her son Jesus, fights against Satan until the end. From Genesis to Revelation, the Bible describes Jesus and Mary *together* crushing the serpent's head. The New Adam and the New Eve are on the same victorious team.

Mary as the New Ark of the Covenant

The Ark was the holiest object in the OT religion. It was sacred because it carried the stone tablets of the Law that God gave Moses at Mount Sinai. In Exodus 25, God gave meticulous instructions for constructing the Ark. It had to be made of acacia wood (supposedly incorruptible), plated inside and outside with pure gold. It had to be kept free from all impurity and profanation. In 2 Samuel 6:6–7, God struck a man named Uzzah dead because he dared to touch the Ark.

From the earliest centuries, Christians saw the OT Ark as a type of Mary.[5] The connection is clear. That Ark carried the *written* Word of God; Mary carried the *living* Word. Mary is

---

[4] As we often say at Mass, "Dying you destroyed our death; rising your restored our life…."

[5] St. Ambrose, for example, details several ways in which The Ark of the Covenant (Ex 26:33, 40:20) prefigured Mary: "The Ark contained the Tables of the Law; Mary contained in her womb the heir of the Testament. The Ark bore the Law; Mary bore the Gospel. The Ark made the voice of God heard; Mary gave us the very Word of God. The Ark shown forth with the purest of gold; Mary shown forth both inwardly and outwardly with the

the living Ark of the living Word. The Ark helps us to see the biblical basis for doctrines like the Assumption, which are not taught *explicitly* in Sacred Scripture, but which are taught *implicitly* through typology.

MARY AS THE NT QUEEN MOTHER

The OT kings clearly prefigured Jesus Christ, the NT King of kings (Revelation 19:16). Jesus, in His humanity, descended from King David. Therefore, the kings of Judah, who were from David's line, especially prefigure Jesus' kingship. Luke 1:32 says, "the Lord God will give to him [Jesus] the throne of his father David."

Interestingly, the *wife* of the king of Judah was *not* the queen. The queen was the king's *mother*. She was known as the Queen Mother. She had great honor and authority in the kingdom. In 1 Kings 2:19–20 we read:

> So Bathseba went to king Solomon, to speak to him on behalf of Adonijah. And the king rose to meet her, and bowed down to her; and he sat on his throne, and had a seat brought the king's mother; and she sat on his right. Then she said, "I have one small request to make of you; do not refuse me." And the king said to her: "Make your request, my mother; for I will not refuse you."[6]

By honoring his mother and giving her a throne at his right hand, Solomon established an institution that lasted as long as the kings of Judah, nearly four hundred years. The Queen Mother served as the king's confidant and advisor. The Queen Mother had an official position; she had to be deposed in order to be removed (1 Kings 15:13). The Jewish idea of Davidic kings would have naturally included the king on his throne with the queen mother at his right hand.

The Holy Spirit, in leading the OT people of Judah to establish the office of Queen Mother, was preparing the way for Mary. Jesus, the NT Davidic King, does not have a wife. His mother would be the NT queen. This is exactly what Revelation 11 and 12 describe. A woman (Mary) gives birth to a son (Jesus) who will "rule all the nations" (12:5). Jesus is a new Solomon. Just as Solomon ruled over other kings (2 Chronicles 9:23–26), Jesus is the "King of kings and Lord of lords" (Revelation 19:16).

Just as Solomon, son of David, built a Temple housing the Ark of the Covenant (the Temple was destroyed and the Ark lost in 587 BC), Jesus, son of David, builds an eternal Temple housing a new Ark of the Covenant in heaven (11:19). And just as King Solomon enthroned his queen mother at his right hand, Jesus enthrones Mary as His Queen Mother: "a woman clothed with the sun, with the moon under her feet, and on her head a crown of twelve stars" (Revelation 12:1).

Any king of the house of David would be expected to have a queen mother. That's precisely what Mary is: the Queen Mother of the Messianic King.

By studying the great honor and dignity queen mothers had in the OT, we can appreciate the profound role God has given Mary as the NT Queen Mother.

---

splendor of virginity. The gold which adorned the Ark came from the interior of the earth; the gold with which Mary shone forth came from the mines of heaven."

[6] In this particular case, Solomon refused his mother's request as it would have meant civil war.

THE FOUR DEFINED MARIAN DOCTRINES

In our own spiritual lives, Catholics know how important Mary is in leading us to a closer relationship with Jesus. However, when we discuss our faith with non-Catholics, we often avoid talking about Mary because we feel unprepared to explain and defend Marian doctrines. The remedy is simple. With a little study and a lot of charity, we can share our Marian beliefs easily and effectively.

NON-CATHOLIC STUMBLING BLOCKS

Several "stumbling blocks" keep non-Catholics from appreciating Mary:

(1) Thinking in "Either/Or" Categories

Non-Catholic Christians often approach Scripture with an "either/or" mentality. For example, they say you love *either* Jesus *or* Mary; you follow *either* Jesus *or* the Pope.[7] This "either/or" mentality is at the root of most doctrinal differences between Catholicism and Protestantism. Protestants tend to divide what Catholics unite. Their theology pits the Bible against Tradition; faith against works; the invisible communion of believers against the visible Church; the finished work of Christ against sacraments, penance, and Purgatory; prayer to God against prayer to the saints; and the one sacrifice of Calvary against the continuing sacrifice of the Mass.

These are false dichotomies; we must not pit one of God's gifts against another. These pairs are complements, not competitors. The Catholic approach is "both/and": we accept *both* the Bible *and* Tradition, *both* faith *and* works, and all the rest. While the either/or approach can sometimes be valid, it does not apply to Mary. The Bible never places Mary in opposition to Jesus, nor does the Catholic Church. Jesus and Mary are on the same team. As we will show later, the Bible is very clear that we are to show Mary special honor. When we honor Mary, we honor Jesus who gave Mary her privileges. The honor we give to Mary she in turn gives to God (Luke 1:46–55).

(2) Misunderstanding Doctrinal Development

Non-Catholics have a hard time distinguishing the *development* of doctrine (which is valid) from the *change* of doctrine (which is corruption). However, non-Catholics do agree that, in our individual lives, we are constantly gaining deeper insight into our beliefs. They also believe the early Church gained deeper insight into the doctrines of the Trinity and the person of Christ.[8] Since the Church is a living, growing organism (see Matthew 13:31–32) that learns from experience and reflection, it *must* continually grow in its understanding of the deposit of faith. Although the deposit of faith was completed at the end of the apostolic

---

[7] We are indebted to Steve Wood for this and other insights (his highly regarded audiotape, "Mary: World's Greatest Woman," is available from the Family Life Center: 1.800.705.6131).

---

[8] The Church did not define the Trinity, the Christological doctrines (one person, two natures, two wills), or even what books are inspired and belong in the Bible for

age, our understanding of it will grow until the end of time. This development of doctrine applies to Marian beliefs just as it does to the rest of our faith.

(3) Confusing Doctrinal Definition with Doctrinal Invention

Many think the Church *creates* doctrines when she dogmatically defines them. Thus, they believe the Church *created* the doctrine of the Assumption when she defined it in 1950. The Catholic Church teaches that public revelation ended with the death of the last Apostle (about AD 100). Thus, there can be *no new doctrines*. When the Church defines a dogma like the Assumption, she is using her Christ-given, infallible authority to declare this particular belief is part of the original deposit of faith, and thus *must* be believed by all Christians.

(4) Restricting God's Word to Sola Scriptura

Protestants aggressively challenge Marian doctrines with their "Bible alone" idea. *Sola scriptura* is the lens through which they view all religious questions. Some Marian beliefs depend for their fullness on Sacred Tradition. To dialogue effectively with non-Catholics about Mary, you must first refute *sola scriptura*.[9] After refuting *sola scriptura*,

you can then establish the solid biblical and historical basis for Marian beliefs using this booklet.

(5) Failing to Appreciate Typology

Protestants often fail to see that the OT teaches many things about Mary through types. We explained typology on page 4. By emphasizing Mary's roles as the new Eve, the new Ark of the Covenant, and the NT Queen Mother, we can show the biblical foundations for Marian beliefs. Mary's role as the NT Queen Mother is especially important for helping Protestants understand Marian devotions. Once we demonstrate from Sacred Scripture that Mary is our spiritual mother and heavenly queen, our modern Marian prayers and devotions will start to make sense.

Many Protestants will not find the arguments in this booklet convincing because they have deep-seated antipathy to our Marian doctrines and demand to see things *explicitly* spelled out in Scripture. Point out that many beliefs they accept—such as the Trinity, the canon of the Bible, and the death of the last Apostle closing the deposit of faith—cannot be found explicitly in the Bible. As a last resort, remind them that Christians ultimately must submit to Church authority in matters of doctrine. Our first booklet, *Beginning Apologetics 1*, demonstrates the authority of Christ's Church, and why this authoritative Church is the Roman Catholic Church.

---

hundreds of years after Christ. Nevertheless, all Christians accept these as a matter of faith. Therefore, all Christians must accept that legitimate doctrinal development can occur. To reject doctrinal development is to reject the Bible and fundamental Christian beliefs.

9 See page 13 of *Beginning Apologetics 1* for a short refutation of *sola scriptura*. See *Beginning Apologetics 7: How to Read the Bible* for a longer

treatment. For a great detailed refutation of *sola scriptura*, see Mark P. Shea's *By What Authority? An Evangelical Discovers Catholic Tradition* (Huntington, IN: Our Sunday Visitor, 1996).

MOTHER OF GOD

Non-Catholics think we give the Blessed Virgin Mary too much honor. They reject the four defined doctrines of Our Lady: her *Divine Maternity* (that Mary is the Mother of God); her *Perpetual Virginity* (that Mary remained a virgin her entire life); her *Bodily Assumption*; and her *Immaculate Conception*.

Non-Catholics often want to dispute Marian beliefs immediately. Insist on starting with more *basic* differences: Apostolic authority, the Real Presence of Christ in the Eucharist, or the "Bible alone" idea. However, you should be prepared to eventually explain and defend Mary.

Catholics believe four defined doctrines about Mary. She is:

① Mother of God
② A Perpetual Virgin
③ Bodily Assumed into Heaven
④ Immaculately Conceived

Before discussing the four major doctrines, ask why it is wrong to honor the mother of our Savior. God honored her above all creatures by making her the mother of His Son. In honoring Mary, the Catholic Church is following the example of God Himself. Mary's special privileges were given to her by God, not man.

In **Luke 1:26–56**, Archangel Gabriel's greeting shows Mary great honor. Elizabeth, "filled with the Holy Spirit," twice calls Mary blessed in just four short verses. Guided by the Holy Spirit, Elizabeth honors Our Lady saying, "why is this granted me, that the *mother of my Lord* should come to me?"

In verse 48, Our Lady prophesies that *all ages* will call her blessed. Ask non-Catholics why they don't call her Blessed Virgin Mary as Catholics do. They call her Mary or perhaps Virgin Mary, but almost never *Blessed* Virgin Mary. Let them see it is Catholics who are being biblical here.

Having established the biblical basis for honoring Our Lady, you can begin discussing the four major Marian doctrines. Don't try to deal with all four doctrines at once. This takes a lot of time and involves many difficulties and side issues. For apologetic purposes, focus on Mary's title of Mother of God for these reasons:

(1) This is her first and greatest privilege; the other privileges follow from it. If they can accept this doctrine, they will grasp the others more readily.

(2) It is the easiest to defend doctrinally, biblically, and historically.

(3) Each of the three great pillars of the Reformation—Martin Luther, John Calvin, and Ulrich Zwingli—accepted this doctrine wholeheartedly.

Most Protestants are shocked to learn that the founders of Protestantism *insisted on honoring Mary as Mother of God and Ever-Virgin* (see page 12 and page 18).

Reason Demands that Mary is the Mother of God

All Christians believe that Jesus was born of the Blessed Virgin Mary. They also believe that although Jesus has two *natures* (divine and human), He is one Divine *Person*. Since this *one Person* was born of Mary, she truly is the Mother of the *one Divine Person*: in short, the Mother of God.

The logic is simple:

(1) Mary is the mother of Jesus.

(2) Jesus is God.

(3) Therefore, Mary is the Mother of God.

If one denies Mary is the Mother of God, whether he realizes it or not, he is *denying the Incarnation*. He is saying either that Jesus is not God, or that Jesus is two persons: one human, one divine. Non-Catholics ask: "How can Mary, a *creature*, be the mother of the *Creator*?" When the eternal Son of God became man, He assumed a human nature. Thus He could be born of a woman just as we are.

Scripture Teaches that Mary is "Mother of God"

Luke 1:43: Elizabeth calls Mary "mother of my *Lord*." In the NT, "Lord" refers only to God.

Matthew 1:23: "'Behold, a virgin shall conceive and bear a son, and his name shall be called Emmanuel,' (which means *God with us*)."

Luke 1:35: "the child to be born will be called holy, the *Son of God*."

Galatians 4:4: "when the time had fully come, God sent forth his Son, *born of woman*."

Early Church Fathers Confirm Mary's Divine Maternity

St. Ignatius of Antioch (110): "For our *God*, Jesus Christ, *was conceived by Mary* in accord with God's plan…."[10]

St. Irenaeus of Lyons (180–199): "The Virgin Mary … being obedient to His word, received from an angel the glad tidings that *she would bear God*."[11]

Church history shows that Mary's title of Mother of God was not rejected until 429. In that year a bishop named Nestorius promoted the heresy that Jesus is *two distinct persons*, and that Mary is the mother of the human person only. In 431, the Council of Ephesus condemned this heresy. It did not surface again in Christianity until after the Reformation. The Nestorian heresy shows that correct belief about Mary preserves correct belief about Jesus.

Protestants' unwillingness to acknowledge Mary as the Mother of God is a radical departure from Sacred Scripture and the Fathers. It also implies that Jesus is either not God, or that He is two persons, both of which are heresies.

---

10 *Letter to the Ephesians*, 18, 2; William A. Jurgens, editor, *The Faith of the Early Fathers* (Collegeville, MN: Liturgical Press, 1970), Volume 1, #42.

11 *Against Heresies*, 5, 19, 1; Jurgens, Volume 1, #256a.

Protestant Reformers Insist that Mary is the Mother of God

Martin Luther: "In this work whereby she was made the *Mother of God*, so many and such good things were given her that no one can grasp them…. Not only was Mary the mother of Him who is born [in Bethlehem], but of Him who, before the world, was eternally born of the Father, from a Mother in time and at the same time man and God."[12]

John Calvin: "It cannot be denied that God in choosing and destining Mary to be the Mother of His Son, granted her the highest honor…. Elizabeth calls Mary Mother of the Lord, because the unity of the person in the two natures of Christ was such that she could have said that *the mortal man engendered in the womb of Mary was at the same time the eternal God*."[13]

Ulrich Zwingli: "It was given to her what belongs to no creature, that in the flesh *she should bring forth the Son of God*."[14]

Protestants claim that because Mary could not have given Jesus His divinity, she cannot properly be called His mother. This is a serious error. Jesus is ONE person. A person is a unity. That is why we say a *person* is born, not a nature or a body. For example, our parents did not give us our souls (they are created

directly by God), only our bodies. However, we never say our mothers gave birth only to our *bodies*. Rather, they gave birth to *us*!

Even if Protestants will not accept Mary as the Mother of God, they do agree she is the mother of Jesus. We can use this as a starting point to help them understand Mary's great privilege. We know that a mother's involvement in her child's life is *total*. She carries that child in her womb, she nurses him, and she is intimately involved in caring for him physically, socially, and spiritually.

We also know that the more important a person is in Christ's mission, the greater honor he has in heaven. That is why, in heaven, the Apostles have such high places (Luke 22:29–30). Mary gave Jesus His body, which was the instrument of our redemption. She carried Him in her womb, nursed Him, clothed Him, fed Him, and protected Him. In all ways, Mary consented to the Father's will for Jesus. She even accompanied Jesus to Calvary where she participated profoundly in His sufferings. These considerations will help Protestants understand why Mary is the greatest of all God's creatures, as the Catholic Church teaches.

Note that when great Church Fathers like St. Ignatius of Antioch and St. Irenaeus call Mary the Mother of God, they presume Christians take it for granted. They don't see any need to explain and defend this belief as if it were in any way controversial. In the fifth century, when Nestorius began attacking this belief the Church immediately recognized he was presenting something new and heretical.

---

12 Weimer, *The Works of Luther*, English translation by Pelikan, Concordia, St. Louis, Volume 7, 572.

13 *Calvini Opera*, Corpus Reformatorum, Braunschweig-Berlin, 1863–1900, Volume 45, 348 and 335.

14 *Zwingli Opera*, Corpus Reformatorum, Berlin, 1905, in Evang. Luc., Op. Comp., Volume 6, I, 639.

Corollary Doctrine: Mary is Our Spiritual Mother

Even if Protestants will not accept the doctrine of Mary's divine maternity, it may still be possible to convince them Mary is our spiritual mother. If they can accept this, then a lot of Catholic Marian beliefs and devotions will start to make sense.

We have already shown that the queen mothers of the OT prefigure Mary as both mother and queen of the NT chosen people. Early Church Fathers like St. Justin and St. Irenaeus teach that Mary is the New Eve. Since Eve is the mother of the human race in the order of nature, the Fathers saw Mary as the mother of the human race in the order of grace. The prayer *Sub Tuum Praesidium* (around 250) illustrates how the early Church viewed Mary as a spiritual mother:

> We fly to your patronage,
> O Holy Mother of God,
> despise not our petitions
> in our necessities,
> but deliver us from all danger,
> O ever glorious and blessed Virgin.

This beautiful prayer anticipates the *Memorare* of St. Bernard, and demonstrates that early Christians honored and recognized Mary's spiritual maternity.

We believe Mary is the mother of all people because Jesus redeemed the whole human race. She is also the mother of the Church in a special way. If one reflects carefully on who Jesus is, and what role Mary played in His mission, he can see that Mary must have some special maternal role in the Church, the body of Christ. This is what the NT teaches.

Mary As Spiritual Mother in the NT

John 19:26–27. "When Jesus saw his mother, and the disciple whom he loved standing near, he said to his mother, 'Woman, behold your son!' Then he said to the disciple, 'Behold your mother! From that hour the disciple took her to his own home.'" Jesus only spoke seven times from the cross. Here, He is doing more than just making domestic arrangements (although that is certainly part of the literal sense of the text).

The Church has always understood that Jesus was revealing to all beloved disciples, represented by John, that Mary is *our* spiritual mother and that we are *her* spiritual children. In this most solemn context, the climactic moment in salvation history, Jesus' words indicate He is giving an important revelation. Recall the words of John the Baptist: "*Behold the Lamb of God!*" (John 1:29). Just as John is indicating something profound about Jesus, so Jesus is indicating something profound about Mary and her relationship to all of Jesus' beloved disciples.

1 Corinthians 12. In this chapter, St. Paul teaches that the members of the Church are the body of Christ. Christians are not literally part of the *physical* body of Christ. St. Paul is teaching that, through grace, we are spiritually united to Jesus. If Mary is the mother of the literal person of Christ, and if the members of the Church are members of Christ, then Mary is spiritually our mother as well.

14

Hebrews 2:11. "For he who sanctifies and those who are sanctified have all one origin. That is why he is not ashamed to call them brethren...."

If Jesus is not ashamed to call us "brethren," we should not be ashamed to call His mother our mother. After all, we call His Father our Father. Through grace, we get a whole new family, including Mary as our spiritual mother.

Revelation 12. This chapter focuses on the "woman clothed with the sun." Who is this woman? Christians agree that this woman's child is Christ (compare Revelation 12:5 with 19:15–16). Therefore, the woman must be Mary. Symbolically, this woman can also represent the Church and Israel. But *literally* she is Mary since Mary is the only woman who was literally Christ's mother. Revelation 12:17 says the woman has other children: "those who keep the commandments of God and bear testimony to Jesus"—Christians. This woman is the literal mother of Jesus *and* the spiritual mother of all Christians.

St. Paul calls Jesus the new Adam (1 Corinthians 15:45–47). Adam, the natural father of the human race, prefigured Christ, the supernatural father of the human race. The early Fathers applied the same principle to Eve and Mary. Eve, the natural mother of the human race, prefigured Mary, the supernatural mother of the human race. Early Christians saw this clearly, and so should we.

Since a mother's role in her child's life is all-encompassing, Mary has been given a profound role in our lives. Just as fathers on earth reflect in some way the fatherhood of God (Ephesians 3:14–15), mothers on earth reflect Mary's spiritual maternity. Mary's motherhood helps us understand how important a role God has given her in our spiritual lives. We must acknowledge Mary's role and embrace it as a precious gift from God, just as we embrace God's priceless gifts of the Bible and the Church. That is what Catholic Marian devotion is all about.

PERPETUAL VIRGINITY

The Catholic Church teaches that Mary was a virgin before, during, and after the birth of Jesus. All Christians believe Mary was a virgin *before* Jesus' birth and many accept that Mary remained a virgin *during* Jesus' birth. But only a few Protestants believe Mary was *ever-virgin*. Fundamentalists, Mormons, Jehovah's Witnesses, and others immediately challenge Mary's perpetual virginity because they think they have an airtight case against it. You can easily defend this doctrine through Sacred Scripture, the Fathers of the Church, and common sense.

*Mary was to have perfect spiritual **intactness**—sinlessness. God wanted Mary's body to reflect this intactness.*

Besides saying Mary's perpetual virginity is unbiblical, many people believe this doctrine downgrades sex in marriage. The Church has always taught sex is a wonderful gift from God, and that its use within marriage is good and holy.

God specially equipped Mary to be the Mother of God, spouse of the Holy Spirit, the mother of the Church, and a leader in the battle against evil. He preserved her from all sin to enable her to fulfill these roles perfectly and to give her maximum power against Satan. Thus, she was immaculately conceived. Mary was to have perfect spiritual *intactness*—sinlessness. God wanted Mary's *body* to reflect this intactness. That is why God chose to miraculously preserve her virginity when she gave birth to Jesus. He also kept her body from corruption after death (the Assumption). Sacred Scripture teaches that our bodies mirror our spiritual condition. After humanity was spiritually wounded by the Fall, our bodies became subject to death and decay. In heaven, when we will be spiritually perfect, our risen bodies will be perfect as well.

Notice how all the Marian teachings are beautifully interconnected and theologically sound. The doctrine of Mary's perpetual virginity does not downgrade marital sex, but rather reflects Mary's unique role in God's saving plan.

To defend Mary's perpetual virginity, we will first deal with verses used to attack this doctrine. Next, we will look at other verses that defend it. Then, we will examine the teachings of the early Church Fathers. Finally, we will show even the fathers of the Reformation (who invented *sola scriptura*) strongly defend this doctrine as biblical.

Verses Used to Disprove Mary's Perpetual Virginity

Matthew 13:55: "Isn't this the carpenter's son? Isn't Mary known to be his mother and *James, Joseph, Simon, and Judas his brothers*?"

In biblical times, as in our own, the word "brother" is used in many ways. It can indicate sibling, relative, friend, or associate. In Acts, fellow Christians are called brothers (Acts 21:7) as are Jewish leaders (Acts 22:1). In the original Hebrew, Genesis 14:14

calls Lot the "brother" of Abraham when in fact, Lot was Abraham's nephew (Genesis 11:26–28). For this reason, many modern translations simply use the word "nephew" or "kinsman" for "brother" because that is what the Hebrew word for brother indicates. To determine the exact relationship of Jesus' "brothers," we must examine other verses to get a fuller picture. Matthew 27:56 and Mark 15:40 tell us that two of these "brothers," James and Joseph, are sons of *another* Mary, not the mother of Jesus. John 19:25 identifies this other Mary as the wife of Clopas.[15]

Objection: The word for "brothers," *adelphoi*, is a precise Greek word that literally means "from the same womb." So these brothers must be uterine-brothers.

Answer: Our English word "brother" literally means "from the same parents" and yet we apply it to all sorts of other relationships: "brothers in arms," "brothers in Christ," relatives, friends, and so on. Likewise, the Jews used this specific Greek word to refer both to blood-brothers as well as to other relationships (see Mt 23:8 and Acts 7:23). Consider 1 Corinthians 15:6, where St. Paul says that Jesus "appeared to more than *five hundred brethren* [*adelphoi*] at one time." If all five hundred were "from the same womb" then that was some miraculous mother! The same holds true for the 120 brethren [*adelphôn*] in Acts 1:15.

Matthew 1:24–25: "Then Joseph being raised from sleep did as the angel of the Lord had bidden him, and took unto him his wife; and he knew her not *till* she had brought forth her *firstborn* son; and he called his name Jesus" (*King James Version*).

Protestants claim these verses give two reasons why Mary was not ever-virgin. The Bible says Joseph abstained from sexual relations with Mary *till* she gave birth to Jesus. Doesn't "till" imply that *after* she gave birth to Jesus, Mary had normal sexual relations with Joseph? No. The word "till," short for "until," does not necessarily imply a later change of condition (in this case, sexual abstinence). For example, 1 Corinthians 15:25 says that Christ "must reign until he has put all his enemies under his feet." Does this mean that *after* he has put all his enemies under his feet, Christ will cease to reign? No. Christ will reign forever (Luke 1:32–33).[16]

Protestants also maintain that since Jesus is called "*first*born son," Mary must have had other children. This is a serious misunderstanding. "Firstborn" is a legal term indicating a special privilege or rank. Psalm 89:27 calls David "firstborn" even though he was Jesse's eighth son (1 Samuel 16). Colossians 1:15 calls Jesus "the first-born of all creation." Many people were born before Christ. St. Paul is simply indicating that Jesus has primacy over all creatures. Remember, the OT law required all "firstborn" males to be redeemed 40 days

---

15 Significantly, Matthew specifically calls *this* Mary, the Mother of James and Joseph, "the *other* Mary" (Matthew 27:61, 28:1) to distinguish her from—who else?—the first and most obvious Mary the reader will think of: Mary, the Mother of Jesus.

16 In many verses, "until" does *not* imply a subsequent change of condition: Matthew 28:20, 1 Timothy 4:13, 6:14; Romans 8:22; Philippians 1:5; Genesis 8:5, 49:10; 2 Samuel 20:3, Judith 12:14, 16:23.

after birth (Exodus 34:20), when a woman couldn't know if she would have other children. She still called him her "firstborn son," even if he turned out to be her only child. The use of the term "firstborn son" in Matthew 1:25 does not prove that Mary had other children.

Verses Used to Defend Mary's Perpetual Virginity

Keep the following two points in mind as we examine Bible passages to defend Mary's perpetual virginity:

(1) The "brothers" of Jesus are *never* called "sons of Mary."

(2) Some of these "brothers" advise and reprimand Jesus (John 7:3–4, Mark 3:21). In Jewish culture, younger brothers *never* admonish an elder brother. Therefore, they could not have been younger children of Mary.

Matthew 15 and John 19:27. In Matthew chapter 15, Jesus vehemently condemns the Pharisees because they had a procedure, the Korban rule, that allowed children to avoid taking care of their parents. In the OT, children had a solemn obligation to care for their elderly parents. This is why the Pharisees' scheme to let people shirk this responsibility made Jesus so angry.

Turn to John 19:26–27 and the scene at the cross. Jesus is about to die. Apparently, Joseph had already died because he is no longer mentioned after Jesus begins His ministry. Mary is in danger of being left alone, so He entrusts her to John the Apostle, Zebedee's son, who was not a sibling of Our Lord. If Jesus had younger siblings, as Protestants claim, His behavior makes no sense. Jesus had condemned the Pharisees for dispensing people from the responsibility of caring for their parents. Why would He dispense His own siblings from this important obligation? Such inconsistency is inconceivable.

Acts 1:13–14:

> When they had entered, they went up to the upper room, where they were staying, Peter and John and James and Andrew, Philip and Thomas, Bartholomew and Matthew, James the son of Alphaeus and Simon the Zealot and Judas the son of James. All these with one accord devoted themselves to prayer, together with the women and Mary the mother of Jesus, and with his brethren.

After the Ascension, the followers of Jesus—including Mary, John the Apostle with whom Mary now lived, and the brothers of Jesus—gathered in the Upper Room. If these brothers of Jesus were also Mary's sons, Mary would be praying together with her sons who were faithful followers of Jesus, and yet going home with John. In her Jewish culture, such a situation simply would not happen.

A careful reading of the Bible supports the Catholic doctrine that Mary had no other children because she was ever-virgin. Now let's examine what the Church Fathers had to say about this belief.

The Church Fathers Defended Mary's Perpetual Virginity

St. Athanasius, the great doctor of the Incarnation who led the fight against Arianism, is highly respected by Protestants. In his *Discourses Against the Arians*, he explicitly calls Mary "Ever-Virgin."[17] He mentions this title as something Christians take for granted, not as something novel or needing a defense.

At the end of the fourth century, when Helvidius questioned Mary's perpetual virginity, the Church Fathers reacted with outrage. St. Jerome penned a scathing defense, *The Perpetual Virginity of the Blessed Virgin Mary Against Helvidius*, condemning his teaching as novel and heretical. Both St. Augustine and St. Ambrose strongly defended Mary's perpetual virginity.[18] Augustine calls her, "A Virgin conceiving, a Virgin bearing, a Virgin pregnant, a Virgin bringing forth, *a Virgin perpetual.*"

Typology

Earlier we showed that the OT Ark prefigured Mary. God insisted that this Ark be without stain or defect because it was to carry the written Word of God. Even more would God want to preserve Mary, the NT Ark who carried the Living Word of God, from all stain or defect.

Protestant Reformers Defended Mary as "Ever-Virgin"

In conclusion, we can show Protestants how even the founders of Protestantism strongly upheld the doctrine of Mary as "Ever-Virgin":

Luther: "It is an article of faith that Mary is Mother of the Lord and still a virgin…. Christ, we believe, came forth from a womb left perfectly intact."[19]

Calvin: "There have been certain folk who have wished to suggest from this passage [Matthew 1:25] that the Virgin Mary had other children than the Son of God, and that Joseph had then dwelt with her later; *but what folly this is*! For the gospel writer did not wish to record what happened afterwards; he simply wished to make clear Joseph's obedience and to show that Joseph had been well and truly assured that it was God who had sent His angel to Mary. *He had therefore never dwelt with her nor had he shared her company….* And besides this Our Lord Jesus Christ is called the first-born. This is not because there was a second or a third, but because the gospel writer is paying regard to the precedence. Scripture speaks thus of naming the first-born whether or no there was any question of the second."[20]

Zwingli: "I firmly believe that Mary, according to the words of the gospel, as a pure Virgin brought forth for us the Son of God and in childbirth and after childbirth *forever remained a pure, intact Virgin.*"[21]

---

17 *Discourses Against the Arians*, 2, 70; Jurgens, Volume 1, #767a.

18 See *Sermons*, 186, 1; *Heresies*, 56; Jurgens, Volume 3, #1518 and 1974d.

19 *Works of Luther*, Volume 11, 319–320; Volume 6, 510.

20 Sermon on Matthew 1:22–25, published in 1562.

21 *Zwingli Opera*, Volume 1, 424.

IMMACULATE CONCEPTION

Protestants find the doctrine of Mary's Immaculate Conception difficult to understand, and even more difficult to believe. For many, it is the *hardest* Marian doctrine to accept. If a Catholic can simply explain this doctrine correctly to a Protestant, he will have made important progress.

On December 8, 1854, Pope Pius IX infallibly defined the dogma of the Immaculate Conception in these words:

> The Most Holy Virgin Mary was, in the first moment of her conception, by a unique gift of grace and privilege of Almighty God and in view of the merits of Jesus Christ the Redeemer of mankind, preserved free from all stain of original sin.[22]

Explanation of the Dogma

Three Key Points:

(1) Mary was preserved from original sin from the first moment of her existence. Not only was Mary free from original sin, she was also completely preserved from any *stain* (effects) of original sin. This means she had no corrupt nature.

(2) The Immaculate Conception only deals with Mary's freedom from original sin. However, the Church also teaches the doctrine that Mary was never touched by personal sin. In this section, we will deal with the broader issue of Mary's freedom from all sin. This approach helps apologists deal more effectively with objections.

(3) This privilege was given to Mary in view of Christ's merits. Jesus was Mary's Savior. She was redeemed by Jesus Christ just as we are, except that Mary's redemption was unique: it was a proactive redemption. The fruit of Christ's redemption was applied to *preserve* Mary from sin, as it is applied to us to *remove* sins contracted.

Protestants object to the Immaculate Conception for the following reasons:

(1) They say it cannot be found in Scripture. Moreover, it contradicts Romans 3:23, which says "*all* have sinned and fall short of the glory of God."

(2) They claim this doctrine means that Mary did not need to be redeemed by Jesus. This objection can be answered by using the distinction above between redemption that preserves from sin and redemption that cleanses from sin.

(3) They maintain the early Church Fathers did not teach this doctrine. They note even the great St. Thomas Aquinas (1275–1274) rejected it.

We will first deal with Romans 3:23, and then show how to defend the Immaculate Conception scripturally. Finally, we will address the question of the Fathers and St. Thomas Aquinas.

---

[22] Bull *Ineffabilis Deus.*

Romans 3:23–"ALL have sinned…"

It is evident St. Paul is speaking of *personal* sins people commit, as opposed to original sin we inherit. St. Paul does not mean "all" in an absolute sense, which would include every single person. Some obvious exceptions are Jesus, Adam and Eve before the Fall, and children below the age of reason. Catholics believe Mary is another exception.

Earlier in Romans 3:9–10, St. Paul says, "*all men*, both Jews and Greeks, are under the power of sin, as it is written: '*None is righteous, no, not one*; no one understands, no one seeks for God.'"

St. Paul is quoting Psalm 14. When he quotes the OT, St. Paul always respects the original context. He never twists a verse to mean something opposite from what the author intended. So what did King David mean by, "there is none that does good, no, not one" (verse 3)? David is lamenting widespread rebellion in Israel. David's enemies are not just the Gentile nations, but also *fellow Israelites* such as Absalom and Saul, members of his own covenant family. David is using "all" in the *collective* sense of including large proportions of each *group* (Jews as well as Gentiles), not in the *distributive* sense of including each and every *individual*. We know this because David immediately distinguishes "all the evildoers" from "my people" and "the generation of the righteous." If absolutely "no one" is righteous, how can David possibly refer to "the generation of the righteous"?

St. Paul is using this quote in the same collective, not distributive, sense: Gentiles are not the only group sinning against God; even God's covenant people, the Jews, are rebelling. Likewise, Romans 3:23 uses "all" in a collective, not distributive, sense. St. Paul is saying there is no distinction between circumcised Jews and non-circumcised Gentiles: both groups commit personal sins and both need to be justified by faith.

Even if we look at Romans 5:12 and 5:18–19, where St. Paul teaches that all men inherit the sin of Adam (original sin), we still must admit of exceptions. Jesus, Adam, and Eve are exceptions all Christians would acknowledge. Catholics believe Mary, the New Eve, is also an exception.

Scriptural Evidence for Mary's Sinlessness

Genesis 3:15:

> I will put enmity between you and the woman, and between your offspring and hers; He will strike at your head, while you strike at his heel (*New American Bible*).

Interpretation: God is speaking to the serpent (Satan) after Adam and Eve had succumbed to his temptation. The woman's offspring who will strike (crush) the head of the serpent (defeat him) is acknowledged by all Christians to be Jesus. The enmity, or opposition, between the woman and the serpent is the same enmity that exists between Jesus and the serpent. This enmity is *total*; the devil never ensnared Jesus in sin as he did Adam and Eve. Therefore, the woman, the mother of Jesus, would also never be ensnared by sin because she, too, is at total enmity with the serpent. This woman must be Mary.[23] She cannot be Eve, who embraced the devil and turned away from God. Furthermore, Eve did not literally give birth to Jesus, Mary did.

Luke 1:28: The *Revised Standard Version Catholic Edition* (RSVCE), which many consider the best English translation of the Bible, and the *New Vulgate* (NV, the official translation of the Catholic Church) render this verse: "Hail, full of grace" (NV: "Ave, gratia plena").

Interpretation: The angel Gabriel calls Mary "full of grace" to indicate that she has fullness of grace. This would be impossible if Mary were touched by any sin, because every sin diminishes grace. Notice he does not call her "Mary." He substitutes the title "full of grace" for her name to indicate how exceptional and unique Mary's fullness of grace is. If I said, "There goes John, the great tennis player," you know that John is good at tennis. However, if I saw John and said, "There goes *Mr. Tennis*," you'd understand that John is not only good at tennis, but also unique and exceptional in this sport.

Obviously, if Protestants use a version of the Bible that renders Luke 1:28 along the lines of "Rejoice, O highly favored daughter," then this argument will not be as convincing.

---

23 "We are taught that God, Creator of all things, after the sad fall of Adam, addressed the serpent, the tempter and corrupter, in these words, which not a few Fathers, Doctors of the Church and many approved interpreters applied to the Virgin Mother of God: 'I will put enmity between thee and the woman, and thy seed and her seed' (Gn III,15). Now, if at any time the Blessed Mary were destitute of grace even for the briefest moment, because of contamination in her conception by the hereditary stain of sin, there would not have come between her and the serpent that perpetual enmity spoken of from earliest tradition down to [this] time" (Pope Pius XII, *Fulgens Corona*).

Typology Teaches Mary's Sinlessness

In the typology section, we showed how the Ark of the Old Covenant prefigured Mary, the Ark of the New Covenant. The first chapter of Luke's gospel repeatedly makes this connection (see table below).

Church Fathers Teach Mary's Sinlessness

St. Justin Martyr and St. Irenaeus implicitly teach Mary's freedom from all sin when they show her as the new Eve who reversed the first Eve's disobedience. When she disobeyed,

OT Ark	Mary, NT Ark
A cloud of glory covered the Tabernacle and Ark (Exodus 40:34-35; Numbers 9:15).	"And the angel said to her: 'The Holy Spirit will come upon you, and the power of the Most High will overshadow you'" (Luke 1:35).
Ark spent three months in the house of Obededom the Gittite (2 Samuel 6:11).	Mary spent three months in the house of Zechariah and Elizabeth (Luke 1:26, 40).
King David asked: "How can *the ark of the Lord come to me?*" (2 Samuel 6:9).	Elizabeth asked Mary, "why is this granted to me, that *the mother of my Lord should come to me?*" (Luke 1:43).
David *leaped* and danced before the Lord when the Ark arrived in Jerusalem (2 Samuel 6:14–16).	John the Baptist *leaped* for joy in Elizabeth's womb when Mary arrived (Luke 1:44).

As we mentioned, God took great pains to prepare and preserve the vessel that contained His written Word. It was made of enduring acacia wood and pure gold. God demanded that this holy container be without stain or defect. God struck Uzzah dead instantly because he dared to touch, and thus profane, the precious Ark (2 Samuel 6:7). If God took such care to preserve the OT Ark from stain, defect, or profanation, how much more would He carefully preserve the NT Ark, which carried the even holier cargo of the living Word, from all stain of sin?

Eve was free from all sin and concupiscence (the inclination to sin). Thus, her "no" to God was a perfect choice of the will. For Mary's obedience to undo Eve's disobedience, Mary's "yes" to God must be as perfect as Eve's "no." This could only be true if Mary were free from both sin and inclination to sin, just as Eve was. Later Fathers explicitly teach Mary's sinlessness.

St. Ephraim (c. 306–373). St. Ephraim of Syria is a prominent Father and Doctor of the Church. In *The Nisibene Hymns*, he writes:

You [Christ] alone and your Mother
Are more beautiful than any others;
For there is no blemish in you,
Nor any stains upon our Mother.
Who of my children
Can compare in beauty to these?[24]

St. Ambrose (340?–397). St. Ambrose is another important Father and Doctor of the Church. He was instrumental in St. Augustine's conversion. In his *Commentary on Psalm 118,* St. Ambrose writes:

Lift me not up from Sara but from Mary, a Virgin not only undefiled but a Virgin whom grace has made inviolate, free from every stain of sin.[25]

St. Augustine (354–420). Most Protestants respect St. Augustine, whom many consider the greatest of the Fathers. In *Nature and Grace* (415), he writes:

Having excepted the Holy Virgin Mary, concerning whom, on account of the honor of the Lord, I wish to have absolutely no question when treating of sins—for how do we know what abundance of grace for the total overcoming of sin was conferred upon her, who merited to conceive and bear Him in whom there was no sin?[26]

The Question of Original Sin and Mary's Need for a Savior

The Church Fathers held that Sacred Scripture and Sacred Tradition taught Mary's freedom from personal sin. They did not explicitly address Mary's freedom from original sin. In

one passage, St. Augustine implies that Mary was born with original sin. However, he did not explicitly confront this question. He was dealing with another issue and, only in passing, mentions that Mary was freed from original sin at her rebirth (baptism).

In the Middle Ages, the Church Doctors directly tackled the question of Mary and original sin. They all affirmed Mary's life long freedom from personal sin. But theologians like St. Bernard, St. Thomas Aquinas, and St. Bonaventure—each deeply devoted to Mary—saw a difficulty. The Immaculate Conception seems to imply that Mary didn't *need* a Savior. How can we reconcile Mary's freedom from original sin with the universality of Christ's redemption?

These great theologians felt this apparent contradiction had to be resolved before the Church could dogmatically define what the Bible and Tradition appeared to teach: Mary's total sinlessness. Duns Scotus (1266–1308), an English Franciscan theologian, resolved this difficulty. Through his brilliant writings, he proved that Mary's preservation from original sin did not remove Mary's need for a redeemer. It required a *more perfect* redemption: a preservative redemption. If a man pulled you out of quicksand, you would say he saved you. But if he kept you from falling into quicksand in the first place, you would say that he saved you more perfectly.

Christ's merits could obviously be applied to Mary in anticipation. All the OT saints had their sins, including original sin, forgiven in view of the merits of Christ's suffering, death, and resurrection. Once the Church reconciled

[24] *The Nisibene Hymns*, 27, 8; Jurgens, Volume 1, #719.
[25] *Commentary on Psalm 118*, 22, 30; Jurgens, Volume 2, #1314.
[26] *Nature and Grace*, 36, 42; Jurgens, Volume 3, #1794.

Mary's Immaculate Conception with Christ's universal redemption, dispute over this issue virtually ceased.

The Fathers take Mary's freedom from personal sin for granted. The same reasons why God would preserve Mary from personal sin apply even more to original sin. Personal venial sins don't separate a person from God as original sin does.

Mary's role as the New Eve excludes not only all sin, but concupiscence as well. As St. Paul teaches in Romans 5, the gifts won for us by Christ far outweigh the damage done by Adam. God's restoration makes things better than the original. Therefore we should conclude that Mary's "Yes," which led to our redemption in Christ, must have been *more perfect* than Eve's "No," which led to our fall in Adam. Since Eve said no to God with a perfect human nature, Mary likewise must have said yes to God with a perfect human nature. Such a nature excludes all sin and concupiscence.

BODILY ASSUMPTION

On November 1, 1950, Pope Pius XII defined the dogma of Mary's Assumption:

> Mary, the immaculate perpetually Virgin Mother of God, after the completion of her earthly life, was assumed body and soul into the glory of heaven.[27]

---

[27] Apostolic Constitution *Munificentissimus Deus*.

Explanation of the Dogma

This doctrine does not say Mary died. However, the overwhelming tradition of the Church, including the Fathers, is that she did. After Mary completed her earthly life, she was taken into heaven, where both her body and soul were glorified. Mary's body did not undergo corruption.

We distinguish Christ's *Ascension* from Mary's *Assumption*. As God, Christ ascended into heaven by His own power. As a creature, Mary was assumed (drawn up) into heaven by God.

Protestants object strongly to the Assumption as having no basis in Scripture. They also think it contradicts 1 Corinthians 15, where St. Paul teaches that the glorification of the body takes place at the end of time. We will first examine 1 Corinthians 15. Then we will show the biblical basis for the Assumption.

Can Our Bodies be Glorified Before the End of Time?

St. Paul teaches that the bodies of the just will be glorified at the end of time. Does this teaching allow for exceptions? In this same chapter, St. Paul says our bodies cannot enter heaven in their current condition. Our bodies must first become spiritual (glorified). On the other hand, the Bible states that the prophet Elijah was assumed into heaven *with* his body (2 Kings 2:11)—he didn't die! Enoch was also taken to heaven without dying (Genesis 5:24, Hebrews 11:5).

Matthew 27:53 says that after Jesus died and the gates of heaven were opened, the bodies of many OT saints were resurrected. The early Church Fathers taught that these saints' bodies accompanied their souls into heaven. If God assumed the bodies of righteous people like Enoch, Elijah, and the resurrected saints before the end of time, He could certainly grant this privilege to His righteous mother.

Argument from "Intactness"

In the section on typology, we saw that the NT requires us to read the OT in terms of types. We explained how the Ark is a type of Mary. God took care to keep the Ark free from all defect, corruption, and profanation because it carried His *written* Word. Even more would God keep the NT Ark (Mary) free from all defect, corruption, and profanation since her womb carried His *living* Word.

God's desire to keep His Ark *intact* explains why He preserved Mary's virginity even as she gave birth to Jesus, and why He kept her sinless. If God intervened in an extraordinary way to keep His mother physically intact at Jesus' birth, it follows that He would preserve her from bodily corruption at her life's end.

The Ark and the Woman of Revelation 11–12

Turn to Revelation 11 and 12. The seventh angel blows his trumpet, announcing a great victory over the powers of darkness. John sees a vision of the Ark of the Covenant in heaven, and immediately after that, a "woman clothed with the sun." If we ignore the chapter break and follow only the

inspired text, *immediately* after seeing the Ark, John describes Mary—a reminder that Mary *is* the NT Ark. The Ark prefigured Mary's body and soul,

Chapter divisions are not part of the Bible. Stephen Cardinal Langton (1165?–1228) added chapter divisions for our reading convenience.

but it especially prefigured her *body*. She carried the Living Word in her body. What is the Holy Spirit, the Spouse of Mary, telling us in this vision? Mary's *body* is in heaven. He is not giving us the location of the lost Ark.[28] Rather, He is saying that Mary is in heaven body and soul.

Mary's Assumption in the Writings of the Fathers

Explicit teaching by the Church Fathers on the Assumption begins toward the end of the age of the Fathers. Earlier, many apocryphal writings deal with the Assumption. Although these writings are not inspired, it would be a mistake to discount their value altogether. They come from the early centuries of Christianity and reflect ideas popular at the time. Much of what they taught must have been true, or the faithful would never have given them any credibility.

These apocryphal documents describe Mary's transition (Assumption) from earth to heaven. These documents reflect the general belief of early Christians in Mary's Assumption, even if they are not to be pressed too hard in their details. *The Falling Asleep*

28 Jeremiah 3:15–19; 2 Maccabees 1:4–8.

of Mary (also known as the *Assumption of Mary*) comes from around the fourth century and has this account of Mary's bodily assumption:

> the apostles carried the couch, and laid down her [Mary's] precious and holy body in Gethsemane in a new tomb. And behold, a perfume of sweet savour came forth out of the sepulcher of our Lady and mother of God; and for three days the voices of invisible angels were heard glorifying Christ our God, who had been born of her. And when the third day was ended, the voices were no longer heard; and from that time forth all knew that her spotless and precious body had been transferred to paradise.[29]

St. Gregory of Tours. In *Eight Books of Miracles* (575–593), Gregory writes:

> The course of this life having been completed by the Blessed Mary, when now she would be called from the world, all the Apostles came together from their various regions to her house. And when they had heard that she was about to be taken from the world, they kept watch together with her. And behold, the Lord Jesus came with His angels, and taking her soul, He gave it over to the Angel Michael and withdrew. At daybreak, however, the Apostles took up her body on a bier and placed it in a tomb; and they guarded it, expecting the Lord to come. And behold, again the Lord stood by them; and the holy body having been received, He commanded that it be taken in a cloud into paradise.[30]

St. John Damascene (died in 749). St. John Damascene brings the Age of the Fathers to a close. In his *Second Homily on the Dormition of Mary*, he writes:

> Struck by the wonder of the mystery they could only think that He who had been pleased to become incarnate from her in His own Person and to become Man and to be born in the flesh, God the Word, the Lord of Glory, who preserved her virginity intact after parturition [giving birth],—He was pleased even after her departure from life to honor her immaculate and undefiled body with incorruption and with translation [Assumption] prior to the common and universal resurrection.[31]

Neither St. Gregory of Tours nor St. John Damascene treat Mary's Assumption as something novel or controversial. In fact, St. John Damascene gave his homily on Mary's Assumption on the *Feast* of the Assumption![32]

Throughout Church history, no one has claimed to have relics of Mary. Although several cities have competed for the honor of being Mary's place of death, no city has ever claimed to have her body. No one has ever made pilgrimages to her tomb or venerated her bones, as they did for the Apostles and early martyrs.

---

29 Alexander Roberts and James Donaldson, editors, *Ante Nicene Fathers* (Peabody, MA: Hendrickson Publishers, 1994), Volume 8, 591.

30 *Eight Books of Miracles*, 1, 4; Jurgens, Volume 3, #2288a.

31 *Second Homily on the Dormition of Mary*, 10, 18; Jurgens, Volume 3, #2390.

32 As early as the second century, we find Christians expressing their belief in Mary's bodily Assumption. Liturgical feasts celebrating her Assumption begin to appear by the sixth century, and perhaps existed earlier. By the eight century, belief in the Assumption was common among Christians.

ANSWERING COMMON OBJECTIONS

(1) "You Catholics worship Mary. You treat her like a 4th person in the Trinity."

Catholics worship God alone. We do not mistake a creature—even God's greatest creature—for the Creator. We *honor* Mary. Why? Because of the gifts God has given her. By making her His mother, God honored Mary more than we ever could. Scripture calls Mary "blessed" and promises that all generations will do likewise (Luke 1:42, 48). We honor Mary because Jesus honored her (perfectly obeying the 4th commandment) and we are called to imitate Christ.

(2) "You Catholics kneel and pray before statues of Mary. You're worshipping idols."

Do you honestly believe that Catholics can't tell the difference between the God of the universe and painted plaster? Protestants often kneel holding a cross or a Bible. Are they worshipping mere wood or printed paper? No, they will tell you these are reminders of Jesus and His saving deeds. Likewise, images of God's victorious saints remind us of Jesus and His saving deeds. No good Catholic thinks he is worshipping Mary by kneeling before her image in prayer.

(3) "Statues of Mary violate God's commandment not to make graven images (Exodus 20:4–5)."

In Exodus 20:4–5, God prohibits the making of images *for the purpose of worshipping them*. But He does not prohibit making images altogether. In Exodus 25:18–19, God commands Moses to make statues of cherubim. In Numbers 21:8, God tells Moses to make a bronze serpent. The Jews used many carved images in their temple, including angels, oxen, lions, palm trees, and flowers (1 Kings 6 and 7). You probably have pictures in your wallet of your family and loved ones. These are man-made images. Are you worshipping them when you use these images to recall the people they represent? No. This same principle applies to the veneration of statues. Catholics use statues and other images merely to recall the holy people they represent.

(4) "Why do you Catholics pray to Mary? The Bible says Jesus is the 'one mediator between God and man' (1 Timothy 2:5)."

All prayer has God as its object. When we "pray to Mary" we are really praying *to* God *through* Mary. We are asking Mary to intercede and present our petitions to God. Recall how Solomon promised not to refuse any request of Bathsheba, the Queen Mother (1 Kings 2:19–20). Nor will the King of kings refuse the petition of His Queen Mother, just as He did not refuse her request at the wedding feast of Cana (John 2).

Mary's intercession is completely subordinate to, and dependent upon, Jesus' intercession. Read the whole passage (1 Timothy 2:1-8): St. Paul *commands* Christians to intercede for one another. This doesn't go *around* Christ's mediation, but rather *through* it. *Because Jesus is the one mediator between earth and heaven, we as members of Christ's body are able to cooperate with Him as mediators.* We single out Mary's intercession because she is God's most righteous saint and "the prayer of a righteous man has great power in its effects" (James 5:16).

(5) "Mary would have to be divine to hear all the millions of Hail Marys being prayed simultaneously."

Mary doesn't have to be divine to hear multiple prayers. Computers can perform millions of calculations per second. If men can make bits of silicon capable of sophisticated "multi-tasking," it should be child's play for God to make His saints capable of hearing millions of individual prayers. The saints are outside the limitations of space and time because heaven has no space or time. Our earthly way of knowing is limited and incomplete; but our heavenly way of knowing will be full and perfect (1 Corinthians 13:12).

(6) "Jesus disregarded his mother and brothers in Luke 11:27–28 and Matthew 12:46–50. This proves we shouldn't honor Mary."

In these two passages, Jesus is not addressing the question of what honor we should give Mary. Instead, He is correcting the popular mentality that bloodline makes us pleasing to God: "do not presume to say to yourselves, 'We have Abraham as our father'; for I tell you, God is able from these stones to raise up children to Abraham" (Matthew 3:9). Jesus is teaching that *faith* is more important than *biological relationship*, to which Mary would have agreed wholeheartedly. Elsewhere, the Bible shows the tremendous honor due Mary because of her faithful role in salvation history.

(7) "Jesus calls Mary 'woman' (John 2:4, 19:26). Isn't this a term of disrespect?"

No. Showing public disrespect to a parent is a sin against the 4th commandment. In Israel, such disrespect was punishable by death. We know Jesus was sinless (Hebrews 4:16). Jesus is calling Mary the "woman" of Genesis 3:15. Mary is *the* prophetic woman who, with her Son, will crush the serpent's head. That's why He calls her "woman" again at Calvary (skull-place), where Jesus crushes Satan's power. Mary is the obedient woman who undoes the first woman's disobedience. Eve is the natural mother of all the living. Mary is the New Eve, the supernatural mother of all who live in Christ. Mary is the "woman" described in Revelation 12, the mother of the Church who wages war against the dragon. Far from showing her disrespect, Jesus is honoring Mary as the cosmically important "woman" who cooperates with Christ in destroying sin and death.

(8) *"The Catholic Church invented the doctrines of the Immaculate Conception in 1854 and the Bodily Assumption in 1950."*

When the Catholic Church defines a doctrine, she is merely codifying a belief that has always existed in the Church. She did this in 325 when she defined the doctrine of the Trinity and in 382 when she determined the canon of the Bible. But no Christian thinks that she "invented" the Trinity or the Bible when she defined them. Likewise, the Immaculate Conception and the Assumption belong to the deposit of faith. They are taught implicitly through OT typology and explicitly by the Church Fathers.

(9) *"Catholics repeat many prayers in the Rosary. In Matthew 6:7, Jesus condemns repetitious prayer."*

Jesus is not condemning *all* repeated prayer, just prayer repeated "*as the Gentiles do*; for they think that they will be heard for their many words." See 1 Kings 18:25–29 for an example of this pagan mentality that mere repetition will force their god to respond. If *all* repetition is wrong, you could say the Our Father only once in your life! Jesus repeats the same prayer three times in the Garden of Gethsemane (Matthew 26:44). The humble publican who repeated "O God, be merciful to me, a sinner" went home justified, while the proud Pharisee who prayed extemporaneously did not (Luke 18:10–14). The four living creatures in heaven repeat their prayer day and night (Revelation 4:8). Psalm 136 is a highly repetitious litany that is inspired by God! The Bible is unmistakable: prayer repeated with the proper attitude is very pleasing to God.

(10) *"Catholics are superstitious for believing that medals of Mary and relics of saints can perform miracles."*

The Catholic Church teaches that only God can perform a true miracle. But we also know that God can act either *directly* or *through* secondary agents, like people. God sometimes even performs miracles through inanimate objects in order to show the intercessory power of a particular saint. A man came back to life when he contacted the bones of the holy prophet Elisha (2 Kings 13:20–21). God performed miraculous cures through Peter's shadow (Act 5:15–16) and through handkerchiefs that had touched St. Paul (Acts 19:11–12), showing the great intercessory power of St. Peter and St. Paul. Medals of Our Lady and relics of saints have no power to cause miracles in themselves. Rather, God performs miracles *through* these medals and relics to show the great intercessory power of Mary and the saints.

THE ROSARY

The Rosary is a powerful devotion to Mary, popularized by St. Dominic (1170?–1221). Rosary beads are divided into five decades, consisting of one large bead and ten small beads. While saying the prayers, we meditate on the chief events (called mysteries) of Christ's life and Mary's. There are many good pamphlets detailing how to pray the Rosary and meditate on the joyful, sorrowful, glorious and luminous mysteries.

THE MYSTERIES OF THE ROSARY

❧ The Joyful Mysteries

(recommended for Monday and Saturday)

1. The Annunciation
2. The Visitation
3. The Nativity
4. The Presentation of Jesus in the Temple
5. The Finding of Jesus in the Temple

❧ The Luminous Mysteries

(recommended for Thursday)

1. The Baptism of Jesus in the Jordan
2. The Wedding at Cana
3. The Proclamation of the Kingdom of God
4. The Transfiguration
5. The Institution of the Eucharist

❧ The Sorrowful Mysteries

(recommended for Tuesday and Friday)

1. The Agony of Jesus in the Garden
2. The Scourging at the Pillar
3. The Crowning with Thorns
4. The Carrying of the Cross
5. The Crucifixion

❧ The Glorious Mysteries

(recommended for Wednesday and Sunday)

1. The Resurrection
2. The Ascension
3. The Descent of the Holy Spirit
4. The Assumption of Mary
5. The Coronation of Mary

PRAYERS OF THE ROSARY

❧ The Apostles' Creed

I believe in God, the Father Almighty, Creator of heaven and earth, and in Jesus Christ, His only Son, Our Lord; Who was conceived by the Holy Spirit, and born of the Virgin Mary, suffered under Pontius Pilate, was crucified, died and was buried. He descended into hell. On the third day He arose again from the dead; He ascended into heaven and is seated at the right hand of the Father. From thence He shall come to judge the living and the dead. I believe in the Holy Spirit, the holy catholic church, the communion of saints, the forgiveness of sins, the resurrection of the body, and life ever-lasting. Amen.

❧ Our Father

Our Father, Who art in heaven, hallowed be Thy Name; Thy kingdom come; Thy will be done on earth as it is in heaven. Give us this day our daily bread; and forgive us our trespasses as we forgive those who trespass against us; and lead us not into temptation, but deliver us from evil. Amen.

❧ Hail Mary

Hail Mary, full of grace! The Lord is with thee; blessed art thou amongst women, and blessed is the fruit of thy womb, Jesus. Holy Mary, Mother of God, pray for us sinners, now and at the hour of our death. Amen.

❧ Glory Be to the Father

Glory be to the Father, and to the Son, and to the Holy Spirit. As it was in the beginning, is now, and ever shall be, world without end. Amen.

❧ Hail, Holy Queen

Hail, Holy Queen, Mother of Mercy, our life, our sweetness and our hope! To thee do we cry, poor banished children of Eve. To thee do we send up our sighs, mourning and weeping in this valley of tears. Turn then, O most gracious advocate, thine eyes of mercy towards us, and after this our exile, show unto us the blessed fruit of thy womb, Jesus. O clement, O loving, O sweet Virgin Mary.

V: Pray for us, O Holy Mother of God.
R: That we may be made worthy of the promises of Christ. Amen.

❧ Memorare

Remember, O most gracious Virgin Mary, that never was it known that anyone who fled to thy protection, implored thy help or sought thy intercession was left unaided. Inspired by this confidence, we fly unto thee, O Virgin of virgins, our mother. To thee we come, before thee we stand, sinful and sorrowful. O Mother of the Word incarnate, despise not our petitions, but in thy mercy hear and answer us. Amen.

❧ Prayer after the Rosary

O God, whose only-begotten Son, by His life, death and resurrection, has purchased for us the rewards of eternal life; grant, we beseech Thee, that meditating upon these mysteries of the most holy rosary of the Blessed Virgin Mary, we may imitate what they contain and obtain what they promise, through the same Christ our Lord. Amen.

HOW TO PRAY THE ROSARY

1. Say the Apostles Creed and the Our Father.
2. Say three Hail Marys for the intention of an increase of faith, hope and charity.
3. Say the Glory Be to the Father.
4. Announce the First Mystery, then say the Our Father.
5. Say ten Hail Marys.
6. Say the Glory Be to the Father.
7. Announce the Second Mystery, then say the Our Father, ten Hail Marys, and one Glory Be.
8. Announce the Third Mystery, then say the Our Father, ten Hail Marys, and one Glory Be.
9. Announce the Fourth Mystery, then say the Our Father, ten Hail Marys, and one Glory Be.
10. Announce the Fifth Mystery, then say the Our Father, ten Hail Marys, and one Glory Be.
11. Conclude by reciting the Hail, Holy Queen and Memorare.

AVAILABLE FROM
San Juan Catholic Seminars

Call for latest booklets available in Spanish!
All prices subject to change without notice.